W9-CFJ-690

GRACE
INTOXICATED

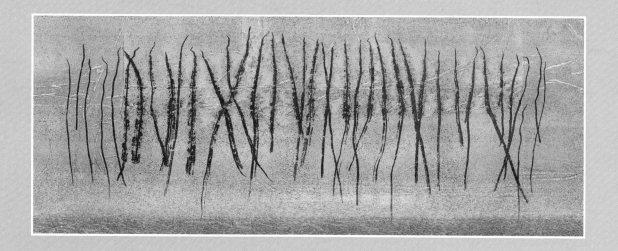

KYLE ELDEN

GRATITUDE

To Shelia Packa, Gary Boelhower and Pamela Mittlefehldt for insight, guidance, critique and encouragement in our weekly poetry group. To my first poetry group Rachel Mock, Tera Freese and Jennifer Derrick for the years of sharing our work and growing together as poets. To Shelia Packa for reading, editing, providing suggestions and insight on the entire manuscript. To Shelia Packa and Kathy McTavish for continued encouragement, guidance, wisdom and willingness to support me as a poet and a published author. To Kate Whittaker for her beautiful paintings and collaboration. To Amy Jutila for proofreading and feedback on the entire manuscript. To Sam Black for believing in my work. To Cecilia Lieder for supporting and believing in this body of work. To Cal Benson for reading, editing and proofreading the entire manuscript and further, for inspiration in the formative years of my life as a writer. To Deb Adele for her support of my poetry and the spiritual teachings that have impacted this work. To my dearest friends who believe in me, love me, support me and provide encouragement through this process and life in general: Billie Schwartz, Amy Jutila, Jillia Pessenda, Andrea Agar, Deb Salzer, Laura Kuettel, Katie Jackman, Gina Farrell, Tony Stensland, Jordan Sundberg, Nicole Abrahamson, Sharon Dawson and Suzi Smith. To my love Jon Heyesen for encouragement, support, love, inspiration, growth and being by my side. To my mom, dad and sisters for all your love and support (Mark Elden, Kathy Hansen, Kacey, Andy and Jody Elden). To my sweet little girl, the light of my life Stella Marais Molina, for teaching me unconditional love, for inspiring and challenging me to become the best person I can be in this lifetime. To Aaron Molina, my daughter's father, for being part of giving me the gift of our daughter and for being an incredible father to her.

To the memory of my dear Grandma Kay whose love for me,
support of my poetry and impact on my life is the catalyst for this book.

ISBN: 978-0-615-69775-8

Library of Congress Control Number: 2012953499

Book design: Kate Whittaker and Kyle Elden. Layout: Kate Whittaker.
Cover image: Superior II. Title page image: Ediacara. Reference list Image: The Marshes.
Printed locally at Pro Print in Duluth, MN.
© 2012 Driftwood Press by Kyle Elden.
© 2012 Art Images and Book Design: Bootheel Press by Kate Whittaker.

PROLOGUE

As artist and writer, we feel our individual bodies of work stand complete and independent of each other. Simply pairing paintings with poems fell short, to our minds, of the true spirit of collaboration. Our explorations into the complex marriage of these two expressive forms helped us discover that by tightly focusing on a poem's essence and finding its mate in a painting's detail, both seemed to coalesce as one upon the page.

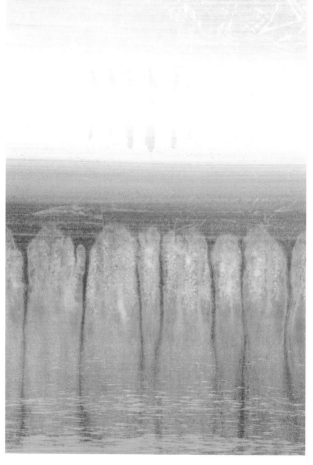

It was a delightful surprise to find how often the act of brush to canvas and pen to paper—our marks and words and their encoded meanings—found symmetry in one another: how signature patterns could mirror an emotive phrase, how timbre (the writer's *and* the reader's) could reveal itself as visual echoes. A stanza might follow the billow of a ship's sail. A vibrant color saturate a verb, become a noun. How visual rhythms find their counterparts in the breath and rest of recitation.

We wish to show how language can be vitally experienced whether one understands the words or is simply, deeply, moved by the gesture of an indecipherable calligraphic mark. Landscapes, ancestral figures, spheres, grace, loss, revelation—all resonate, layer by layer. Their natures are often best revealed in the asymmetry of clear, eloquent words alongside the most elusive of images.

We feel Picasso said it very well, "The artist is a receptacle for the emotions that come from all over the place: from the sky, from the earth, from a scrap of paper, from a passing shape, from a spider's web." We would add that, together, we have transmuted from this receptacle and offered up: a sky catching fire, a hawk called forth, a fading blueprint, an emptied harbor. —*Kate Whittaker and Kyle Elden*

TABLE OF CONTENTS

ORANGE TIGER LILIES

Alongside rotting railroad ties
stacked to enclose this garden
with mostly unruly weeds
these orange Tiger Lilies
come every year
continue to open
their petals shine
dark pollen bursts
from center
abundant and daring
they say to the world
Yes! Yes!
I am alive!

Unashamed of any longing
or desire
they ask for what they need
and graciously receive
sunlight funnels deep into their hearts
roots reach deep into the dirt
and oh so dirty
they call for water
rising up through
succulent green stems

I tell you
they glow
as I walk by today
unhurried
aware
happiness heaves into my body
a great love for life rises
my breath a song of praise

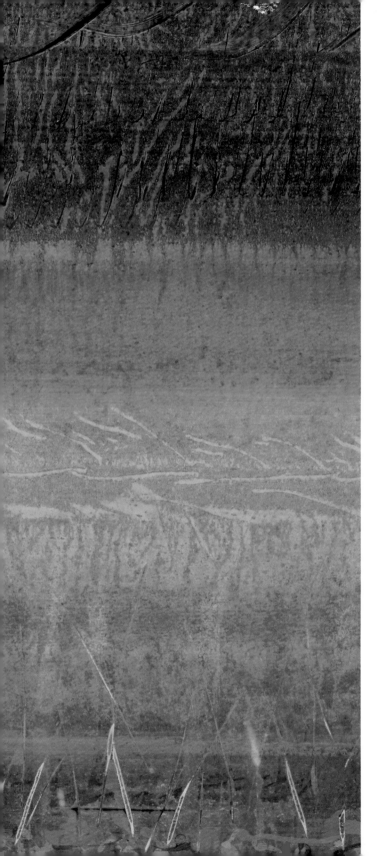

I can only smile
as I cut a russet potato
cooked in olive oil with a dash
of salt and pepper, smile
as I crack eggs and adore
their yellow yokes, smile
as I eat this food in solitude
look out at the lake
filled with moon light
city lights and ships
with shining lights
sweat damp on my body
warm wind wisps through
open window
dances with sheer curtains
this breeze presses against me
cool on my skin
makes me tremble

10

RISING

Don't give your life away to sorrow
to watch its flames take everything
into burning light, to watch the smoke
of your dreams spell out the language
of longing and loss, to hang heavy
in your clothes
and on your hair
forever

If you arrive at this place
and find yourself covered in mud
in this thicket
get down on your knees
mud smudged across your face
dried and cracked on your lips
prayer on your breath
and like the lotus flower
submerged in swamp
rise laughing and red
bright as Jupiter pulling
her many moons
in a tidal dance

DOORWAY

Your palm glides across
this door
the smell of wood and old paint
press against the last thing
between you
and the life
that awaits

Your fingers clasp
cold brass doorknob
and turn, open
light begins to filter in
and you know
it is time

You have learned
what can be learned here

You cannot look back
cannot stay
the past becomes the past

You do the only thing you can do

Words like
regret and
if only
fall like feathers
from a bird in flight
softly floating downward
white
against blue sky

13

FIRE

The sun leaves this day behind
no regrets, doesn't look back
slips down the edge of the lake
sky catching fire
pink flames, pink tendrils of smoke fading
into the dark, dark blue of night closing in
tossing up sparks of stars
she knows how to move through this cycle
knows there is no other choice but to orbit
onward through light and dark
through life and death
knows there is nothing we can hold forever
not inhale, not exhale
not this moment, or that one
not the body
not anybody
not anything
move through the setting
burn through the fire
ash and dust of what was
to rise
resurrect
and shine

THE LONGEST GOODBYE

We knew it was goodbye
the last night you don't want to end
your favorite bar you know you should stop
going to
you know you should leave, but want to stay
again, just for tonight
sit on this same lovely stool
and it's past last call
lights shutting down
the final drops of scotch in your glass
savored—lick the edge, that golden liquid
the heat down your throat, the burn
the glass hitting the counter, pushed away
slides across shadowed surface, cuts through
your reflection
the last dollars laid down
you slip through that same door
the smell of the place on your clothes
on your skin as you walk away
you will dream about
look up, see clear black starry sky
moonbeam a spotlight on you
know it is goodbye
that last drag on the last cigarette
in the last pack, you suck it to the filter
throw it down on wet cement
stare at the burning amber until it fades
stomp it out, taste it on your fingers later
walk home in the drizzling rain, in the dark
with an ache in your heart
tears sloppy on your face
mutter goodbye
as you fall asleep as pink light
cracks open the dawn

THE GIFT

You are the dark oiled mark
a fingerprint of love
forever on me
in my thoughts when all else is quiet
I am alone, still
you are near
although the distance could not
be greater
you never fully left
your spirit formed mine
rearranged, reconstructed, chipped away

In your leaving
I am not a ghost town
vacant, broken down
I am a museum
touched by you
the floor boards worn differently because
of the way you walked across to greet me
to hold me, to love me
our time together, the good
the imperfect
a gift I carry forward
your light within me
around the edges of my life
forever
golden and glowing

BECOMING TEA

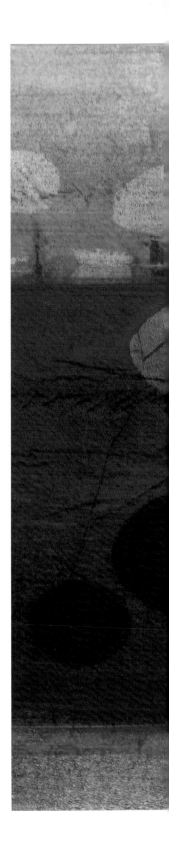

In this red mug
with hot water
a tea bag steeps
releases its golden brown
in swirls
dances
with steam the scent of peppermint
rises, catches the light
a ritual of lips to cup, and
warmth flows gently
cascades down my throat
spreads throughout my body

An act of surrender
so simple
held by a single thread
delicate dark leaves
inside the boundary of tea bag
infused with what is
to transform into something
different
something more
unlocked
released

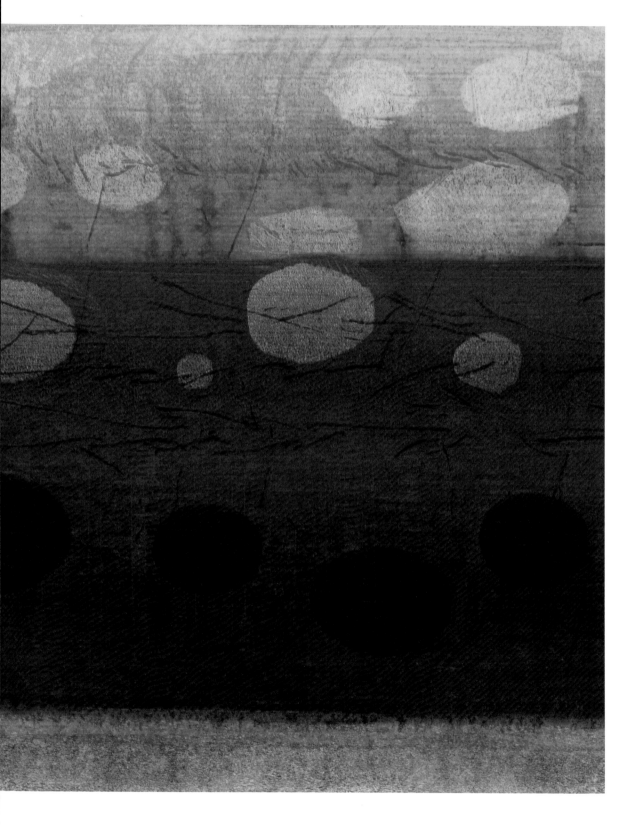

PRAYER

In a prayer you ask
how do you mend a broken heart
tears swell
a giant sun slips away
over the edge of the horizon
pulls the color from the sky

This isn't much like the
glass you broke
kneeling on the floor to pick up
the bigger pieces
carefully placing them in your palm
sweeping tiny shards
until there is no longer
any sign of your clumsiness
of your loss

A broken heart
is this wicked wind you can't see
but whips your hair, slams the door, blows
dirt into your eyes
the memories howl and scream against your windows
blow tree branches to scratch at the side of the house
as you try to sleep, or fry an egg
loss looms like your shadow
follows you wherever you go

Use this pain
imagine yourself bread dough
moist and heavy in the oven
waiting for the right temperature and time
to rise into its fullness

All that we face is holy
so drink this thick dark loss
become grace intoxicated

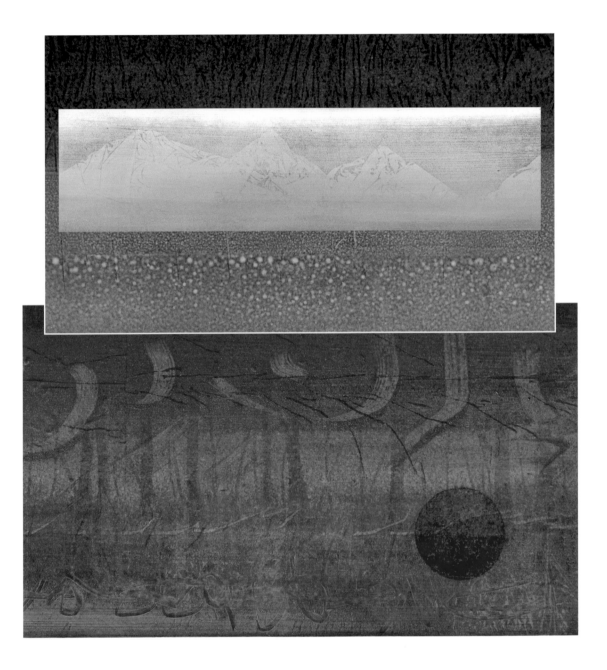

ALL THIS LOVE

With you I wiped off the dust
on all this love
took it down from top shelf
from a back room, back corner
reached through spider web
shadow, patches of light
from a faraway window
once out of reach
a book closed
opened
stories written, stories read
of all this love
all this love with you
all the pages, pages turned
with you I wiped off the dust
moved my hand across hard cover
traced gold lettering of all this love
you couldn't hold
cannot be in this story
and all this love, this love
remains in words and chapters
under golden light of new day
to be devoured, taken in
savored
to be held in strong, warm hands
seen with steady eyes
to be touched with tenderness
and always, always
all this love
with you I wiped off the dust

BEFORE YOU KNOW IT

Before you know it
you smile again
find yourself humming
singing out loud when alone
a prayer of gratitude spills from
your lips as the sunrise
spreads light
across the morning
soaks the sky
the deepest pink
imaginable

You know
the million
ways to hide from your heart
the thousand reasons
to be sad
or scared

But there are more
even more ways to be
alive
more reasons
to move forward
as the hawks are called forth
to migrate, over and over again
to wherever there is more bounty

GRACE

In this nursing home
my grandmother's new home
there are the wanderers and the lost
leaning on walkers
left in wheelchairs
waiting to die

This woman is talking to us now
in her motorized wheelchair
she drives around with a vengeance
like a Harley Davidson motorcycle
still full of fire and life
she has no legs
and brown teeth
and a urine bag protruding
from her blue worn t-shirt
she tells us of adventures
on the DTA
and how she leaves every day
to visit friends or take care
of her son-of-a-bitch ex-husband
who lives at Tri Towers

Another woman
sits in her wheelchair
frail and lanky
wild white hair disheveled
blank stare
cradling a naked baby doll
with a yellow stained abdomen

and red crusted lipstick or nail polish
or who knows what, along the tiny
plastic lips of her child
my grandma asks her "sweetheart
where's your baby's clothes?"
and then whispers to us that
the old coot doesn't ever say a word
but today she stops my daughter
and tells her she has a pretty dress
a very pretty dress
when we walk away my little girl asks me
"why does that lady's baby have a bloody mouth?"

I begin laughing until tears come
and breathe easier
see God's grace in the strangeness
of these people dying awkwardly and too slowly

I'M CRAZY TOO

We are all crazy
in our own way
hiding tiny pieces of
ourselves from the world

I may run along the Lakewalk
at seven and a half minute miles
marked by my Garamin GPS watch
at three in the afternoon
past a picnic table of local drunks
yelling "fuzzzk you bitch"
and "I don't care about anybody, anybody"
smoking Marb 100's, passing around a forty
in seventy degree heat

Running in perfect form
past a woman sleeping on a bench
skin turning red, sweat gleaming
across her cheeks
wearing a knit winter hat
faded black sweatpants
and a navy blue t-shirt
with a ripped up right sleeve
bare feet jut off the edge
years of disappointment
and loss sculpted into the fierce way
she clutches her elixir
wrapped in a brown paper bag
mumbling softly
"you told me you loved me,
you loved me…."

Maybe for a second
I feel good about myself
juxtaposed next to them
their mistakes
their pain on display
like a storefront window
in a shop called CRAZY

Only I partially envy them
with my mistakes, my
neatly packaged pain
hidden from the world

What would it feel like to fall apart
right outside the Biffy
in Canal Park
amidst a swarm of tourists
to yell, and cry, and scream, and pound my fists
on the cement until they bleed
shedding light on my darkest secrets
on my imperfections

DEEP WELL

This is where we know ourselves

arms flung open

laid out

wide wild expanse of sky

body presses against earth

the only sound for miles

is kick drum heartbeat

rising up

from God's deep well

tiny currents hum

waves undulate, unfold

break through

layers of the self

fallen on the landscape

of soul, break open

brown egg shell cracks

opulence cascades

downward until

the golden center

settles

shines

BRIGHT LEAVES

The earth offers its magnificence
even when my heart contracts
against an abyss of grief
that blots hope
like the last shovelful of dirt
thrown over a mahogany casket

Even on this grey day
when winter and autumn collide
most trees are bare and ready
for this coming
but some bright leaves
still cling whole-heartedly
to their lives
radiant on street sides
and in forests miles away

33

34

RIPENING TRICKS

I'm waiting for
our love to ripen

I long to bite into
the soft tenderness
of a nectarine
in 80 degree summer heat
wearing next to nothing
I wipe droplets of sweat
from my forehead
mouth waters
bring it to my lips
the flesh almost
melting from its core
and bite
sweetness explodes
juice drips down my chin
onto my breast
down my hand and arm

This is how I've imagined it
the satisfaction of a perfectly ripe fruit

Not this hopeful waiting
not the hard cold feel to the touch
not the pale colored words spoken
or the silence on your dark
curls, in your brown eyes and long lashes
on your lovable lips and skin

Maybe there's something
I'm missing, a brown paper
bag trick that will help

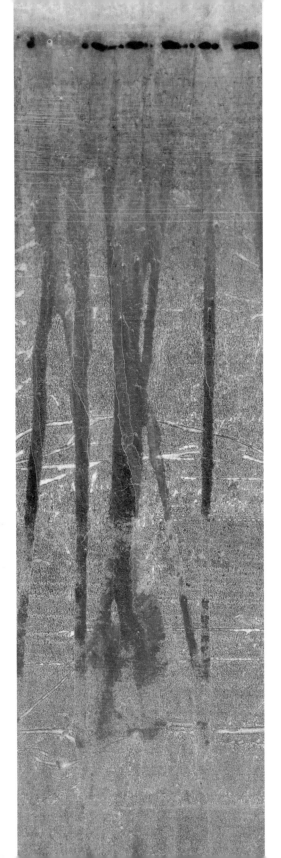

UNRAVELING

I don't remember when the first thread came loose
how it hung like a secret
the words suspended
unspoken
a ripe fruit dangling from its branch

This unraveling began
with silence
moved in like a thick slow rolling fog
and suddenly I can no longer see into
my lover's eyes, even though
we are face to face

I feel myself being pulled downstream
the water diverges and eddies away
I find myself somewhere unfamiliar
unknown

I realize we have ended
and wonder
how it is the buds begin to appear
on empty trees
when all I recall is dead branches
and dirt crusted snow heaps

How it is the lilacs burst open
thrust their sweet scent into the air
forge into this new season
mark this change
as if it were easy

SWEET CHILD

(for Stella)

You came
breaking the darkness
glistening across the lake
beaming summer sunlight
into our lives

You chose us
your parents
whispered to the creator
gently rushing through
the hands of the universe
with the strength
of ocean tides

Inside me
you wove into existence
with the force of cosmos
the planets orbiting
dancing in circles
with the rhythm
of the infinite

Daily you teach us of God
in your smile
when you awake in the morning
full of joy
reminding us how to be
in the present moment
the past
and the future only illusions
of what was and what may come

This world
is crazy and beautiful
it is of both
darkness and light
you will touch pain
and you will touch happiness
both a burning fire
in the heart of
human life

May you always be
in tune with your
true self
always know
you are nothing
less than
miraculous

All the mistakes
and experiences
tumble downward
like autumn leaves
the golden
the red
the orange
the green
the brown
they swirl into
the earth
moving through the cycle
bringing new life
over and over again

GOD

We can only begin
to grasp You
squeezing tiny drops
of the Infinites sweet nectar
golden as dawn's first light
shedding layers of truth
upon humanity

It is through You
upon Your breath
streaming through
branches of trees
swirling out of the
open mouths
of orange poppies and
wildflowers
that life is sustained

Father or King
Mother or Friend
cannot capture You fully
all these names
used to describe You
allow us to be submerged
in the ocean of You
but we have only swam
in the palm of Your
hand, have only heard
whispers of Your wisdom
we do not know
the entirety of You

These metaphors
and beliefs
both give You to us
and tear You to pieces
once a sacred
and still river
Your image is now
broken across that
same water
we must stop
throwing stones
stop fighting
let the waves settle
and wait for You
to emerge clearly

VENUS' FIRE

I am wide open
a cracked egg raw
on cold black frying pan
waiting for heat
to change what is

I try to mold this love
shape winter into summer
but the ice cuts my hands
and blood drops
red on white snow
all around me

The birds are gone
no red-breasted robins
sing easily on
outstretched birch branches

I have sifted through every shadow
taken all possible light

I now hold this darkness
for it has been given to me
as well
I turn from
every urge I have
to wrap it in something
beautiful

I stare deep into
the eyes of the dragon
walk through
Venus' fire
which outshines everything
but the moon

UNDERTOW

The whisper of love
draws me forward
lake currents pull
your touch lures me into
a tangled mess of limbs, skin to skin
and sweat, hair in disarray
looking deep into the blue of your eyes
this trembling memento
burned forever in my heart
a moment I dared to delve into
a slippery fish I caught with my
bare hands and held long enough
to be scale covered and shimmering

OUR SONG

Jose Gonzalez music drones
through tiny speakers
humid summer air and birdsong
seep in through open windows
I taste the sweet salt of
your skin's sweat
only for me
my hands, only for you
move across
soft skin, curve of muscles
our breath sacred, moves rhythmically
blows cool breeze against
hot damp bodies
our song
floats above all others
our song
swept away in deep heaves
of one another
we pull closer, closer
collapse in a tangle of each other
melt into this haze of love

HOW TO SAY GOODBYE

In the morning I wake
no longer in the same bed
in the same house as you

Always before the sun rises
grappling with choices and decisions
that have wrung out our lives
as we have known them together
before the rest of the world begins its day
I face myself in this illustrious unwavering silence
in this darkness
that dawn after dawn
crescendos to daybreak
and all the noise of traffic and other people
who mean well but don't really know our story

There are so many ideas of what it means to love
so much advice *don't give up, fight for love*
you should do this, don't do that

Somehow we migrated together
to our own battlefield
of buried land mines, stockpiles of weapons
somehow the picture we saw of our love
in the beginning never came to fruition
a thousand piece jigsaw puzzle we struggled
to put together with misshapen and missing pieces

This is the time
we have parted
each left in the wake
of waves from a ship
we never quite boarded

How does one say it
goodbye
throbs in my throat
a thistly unfurling finality
a door closes softly for the last time
the wail of a grieving mother
a siren screams down the heart of a city
a heart slows to a stunned stillness
a human soul exits a body

HoME

Jesus, God your name
used to be stones in my mouth
I tried to choke down, or spit out
a dam holds back
a great force of rushing water
I was afraid would swallow me whole
but the Kingdom is greater
than I imagined
there was so much
steam and condensation
I've now wiped away from the mirror
to see myself clearly
to see myself as You do

I have burn marks from the flames of hell
across my body
scars from the casket that held me like a womb
dirt underneath my fingernails from the grave
I've been climbing out of
cuts from rocks and roots I've grabbed
to pull myself up
toward You
the greatest love of my life
God you are everywhere
and within
above and beneath, all around
You were always holding me
wanted me to feel my head against
the beating of Your heart
Your arms wrapped around me
love pouring into me overflowing
glasses of wine and laughter

dancing with me, spinning until

I see stars

singing into daybreak

kissing my forehead

brushing the hair from my eyes

whispering in my ear

"my child, welcome home!"

BLUEPRINT

The blueprints were breathtaking
the potential astonishing
we stared for days at the sleek white paper
at the meticulously drawn lines
of what could be

We were in awe
with all the right materials
stacked neatly next to the
beautifully constructed design
stocked aside the prospect
of something great

We knew this land was riddled
with boulders and jagged rocks, knew
this place was not suitable to build
yet I laid down my precious pearls
and you your precious stones
we began

All that was raised
of this possible masterpiece
crumbled against its foundation

Our ruins
this wood and cement and debris
this once white paper
its delicate blue lines
this topography of us
a precious relic

A DIFFERENT SHORE

A boat adrift
you sailed in
on fire with sunrise
majestic across glimmering
glass water
I pulled you in
held you close
wrapped the rope around the dock cleat and chock
spiraling in overlapping figure eights
around and around the silver anchor
held steady at the shore

Until it snapped, broke apart

I am left
with the short end of the rope
unraveling in the wind

Here
I gather
tiny agates
bright orange
warm as a fiery sunset
I carry in my pocket
for comfort

The silhouette of you
fades into the horizon

Abruptly
I wake from this dream
reach for
what is not there
call your name into
an empty harbor

THIS WATER

I've chased rainbows
cast from shattered bits of life
illusions of light break through shards
sharp illustrious edges
shine like diamonds
the allure calls out all desire
I stomp over shadows
the dark underbelly
the substance upon which I stand
longing to be drenched in color
intoxicated by a mirage
just always ahead
dry throat, unbearable thirst
I drink from empty glasses
try to draw water from broken cisterns
I don't realize
I am already overflowing
with the source of life
this water swirls around all things
rushes into, undulates, pulls back
pools inside
resides

TOOTH FAIRY

Asleep amidst tangled pink comforter
Buttercup your brown and black puppy
Lavender your bald, blue eyed baby doll
and your purple unicorn pillow-pet

Eve of first day of first grade
hot September night moistens
your brown skin with sweat I taste
as I kiss your forehead

I come in with a crumpled dollar bill
in my hand, brush against
your dark curls with my arm
tonight
I am the magic
as I swap tooth for money
beneath pillow
I imagine fireworks
of fairy dust falling from
my fingers

But I know in the morning
your eyes will shine brighter
when you throw your pillow aside
and discover your dollar
you will run to me
fist full of money
gap toothed smile
to crack open my heart
my little girl:
you are the magic

And you'll yell
"mama, mama look!"
And I'll sweep your almost
seven year old, sandy foot,
scraped up knee, dirty fingernail
lipstick-obsessed little self
into my arms
and I'll squeal, and jump around
and dance with you

Because this is better than
any lottery
and I've won more with you
than millions that could afford
yachts, and fancy cars, and
something bigger than our little
apartment

I took that Ziplock baggie
with your small tooth lined
with dried blood
and hid it away in the back
of my desk drawer
under papers and junk
so you won't find out
'til you're older
it was me, and I couldn't
bear to throw away that
little piece of you

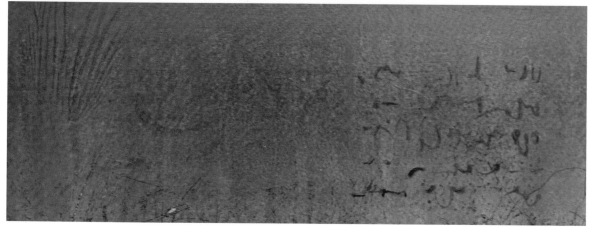

THE CURE FOR DEPRESSION

Get dumb drunk off of sunlight

sing to yourself in buses, hallways

bathrooms, et cetera

fill blank pages with joy of

pen streaking madness

dance naked through your house

go for long walks alone

tongue kiss your dog

don't let anyone take your heart

in their hands to pack it like a snowball

and throw it at a window

so you can watch it melt

against the warmth of something

somewhere else

sing

don't expect anyone to fill

the void inside

be careful with your heart

because it's fragile like ice, glass, or life

and you only get one

life's stubborn sometimes

like thread stuck in a zipper

pick flowers

make daisy wreaths

and wear them in wind-blown

sunbleached hair

forget sunscreen

let your skin burn, peel and curl

like expensive lace

collect odd stones

get high off laughter

and take drags off fresh air

come gather here
because there's nothing broken
that can't be fixed
and we all hold the tools
underneath our ribs
make love with your life
get intimate with a fire
go skinny-dipping and gather goosebumps
don't let the colors fade
this isn't black and white TV
run across rocky back roads
and pavement barefoot
dig deeper into the dirt and
let it stain your fingers
please sing
and cry, but not too much
everything is good
but only in moderation
don't be afraid to look
when you pass a mirror
because you're beautiful
although doctors prescribe
Prozac and Welbutrin
I've heard the best cure
for depression is a nice
tall glass of sunlight

THE CENTER

This is the center of our love
a convergence, a place
where roots unfurl inside gritty dirt
splitting the seed of possibility

This is letting go
not goodbye, but a departure
a place where the tree divides
into branches
reaches for the light
moves toward sky

This is living in the center
of life, a place
where grief and joy
grab us
touch our cheeks
look into our eyes
and kiss our lips
and we fall wildly in love
with our imperfect
and beautiful existence

This is the center
of God, a place
where we stop turning away
stop trying to force the stone
before it is time to be rolled
away from the tomb's entrance
here in this uncertain place
be still, sit in the darkness
and trust that this too
is grace

BROKEN BEAUTY

We learn to be women
look out at the world
magazines, televisions
the horizon of perfection
of airbrushed and
computer masterized images

They tell us
this is what it is
to be beautiful
and all the possibility
whirls in like a fairy
godmother, taps
our young heads
with a sparkling
magic wand

From the time we are small
our minds begin to crumble
before an empire of empty
promises and our dreams
sometimes fold
and are placed carefully
in some bottom drawer
of our hearts

We are given
pounds of fool's gold
to buy our way
into the shininess
and allure of
self hatred

Having once been the
property of fathers
and husbands
we are now mere objects
for gratification
again and again
dismembered
from our humanity

Living east of Eden
the damage has already been done
so push through
the flaming sword
flashing back and forth
to guard the way to the tree
of the knowledge of
good and evil
reclaim the red apple
make vats of
golden juice
and drink up

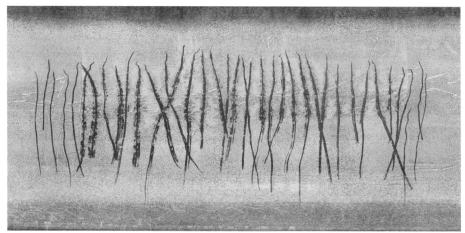

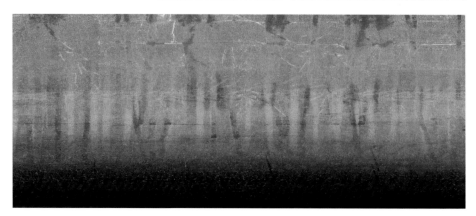

MoVING

I won't
but want to
send you
a package of white tea
a small white towel
maybe a blank piece of white paper
where a poem could have gone
and an empty CD where music
could have been burned
a parting gift
to say goodbye
to have you remember
and maybe laugh
and to signify
the emptiness
that often comes with
moving on
moving
and it's all about
packing boxes
making space
for the new
rearranging
throwing away
what cannot be contained
or held
letting go
moving
moving forward
to a new place
to unpack the things that remain
and place them
neatly, thoughtfully
where they now
belong

THE SUN

Do not stay
at the dark point of the moon
although it's important you visit there

Do not believe this darkness
this emptiness
melancholy flowers
that bloom and die in the same hour
are eternal

Do not give birth to your story
and then carry it around like a dead baby
you cannot bear to bury

Do not resent yourself for your grief
do not hate yourself for that ten pounds
the lack of appetite, the dark circles
from no sleep
for all the tears that swell and fall
evaporate, but the sadness stays

Every day inhale light
slowly begin to orbit
notice the sunshine
the breeze
a child smiling, laughing
the snow
collect moments of happiness

Feel joy
warm and red
begin to beat and flow

Listen to the sweet sound of yourself
shifting gears, driving endlessly
until you are staring into the fierce
face of a full moon
you caught a glimpse of
in your rear view mirror
while you were singing to the radio

You stop
you realize
all along you were the sun
you just couldn't see yourself

IMAGE REFERENCE LIST

The images within this book are details, referenced from the following paintings:

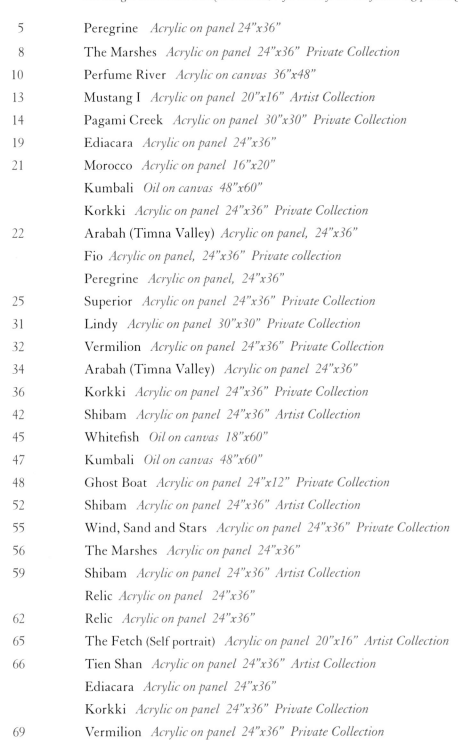